BRITAIN SINCE WORLD WAR II

Health and diet

STEWART ROSS

First published in 2007 by
Franklin Watts
338 Euston Road
London NW1 3BH

Franklin Watts Australia
Level 17/207 Kent Street
Sydney NSW 2000
Copyright © Franklin Watts 2007

Editor: Jeremy Smith
Art director: Jonathan Hair
Design: Jason Anscomb
Picture researcher: Sophie Hartley

Picture credits: Action Press/Rex Features: 25. Alex Segre/Rex
Features: 24l. Antonia Reeves/Science Photo Library: 10b.
C.V.L./Eurelios/Science Photo Library: 22t. Eric Nathan/Alamy:
24r. Getty Images: 6 all, 8b, 9, 19, 20, 21b. Gustoimages/Science
Photo Library: 15t. Homer Sykes/Alamy: 17. Jason Byes/Rex
Features 16r. Juergen Berger/Science Photo Library 26b.
Jonathan Hordle/Rex Features: 26r. Mary Evans/ Ad Lib Studios:
12. Mark Thomas/Science Photo Library: 8t, 11. Michael
Donne/Science Photo Library: 13b. Nick Cobbing/Science
Photo Library: 23b. Paul Vallance: Photofusion: 16l.
Photofusion/Alamy: 13t. Popperfoto: 18r, 21t. RIA
Novosti/Science Photo Library: 15b. Topfoto: 14.
W.A. Ritchie/Roslin Institute/Eurelios/Science Photo Library:
15c. Will & Deni McIntyre/Science Photo Library: 27.

Dewey Classification: 941.085

ISBN: 978 0 7496 7608 7

Printed in China

Franklin Watts is a division of Hachette Children's Books,
an Hachette Livre UK company.

CONTENTS

INTRODUCTION – THE NHS   6

GOING TO HOSPITAL   8

SURGERY   10

GOING TO THE DOCTOR   12

THE MARCH OF SCIENCE   14

THE BAD NEWS   16

HARD TIMES   18

FAST AND FOREIGN   20

GOING GREEN   22

EATING OUT AND LEARNING TO COOK   24

NEW LIVES   26

GLOSSARY   28

FURTHER INFORMATION   29

INDEX   30

In 1945, doctors, dentists, medicines and hospital visits were too expensive for ordinary working people. To solve this problem, in 1948 the government launched the National Health Service (NHS). Its services, paid for by taxes, were free for all.

HEALTH FOR ALL

The NHS was a wonderful idea and admired throughout the world. For the first time ever the British people did not have to worry about the cost when they needed medical treatment. The system was particularly helpful for the poor, elderly and infirm. Many went to the dentist for the first time. The billions of pounds pumped into the NHS helped build better clinics and hospitals. Everyone could benefit from new treatments, like hip replacements, as they were discovered.

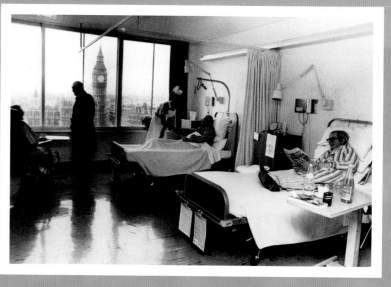

▲ An NHS hospital built in 1976. It offered care for everybody who needed it, not just those who could afford to pay for treatment.

DIFFICULTIES

Managing the NHS was a problem from the start. It was the largest organisation in the country and tremendously expensive. Planners believed it would cost £110 million a year. In fact, in its first year it cost £248 million – over twice as much.

Politicians hoped the cost of the NHS would fall once people had been given the treatment they needed. Nothing could have been more wrong! The cost of the NHS went on rising. By 2006 it was £42 billion a year.

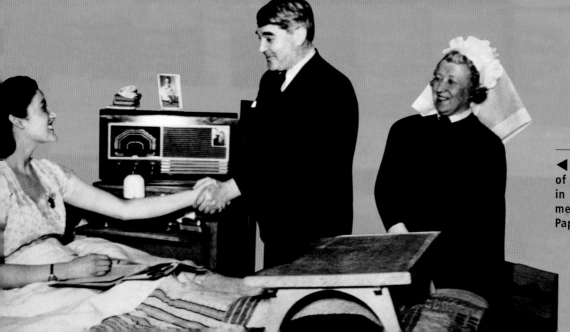

◄ Aneurin Bevan, Minister of Health, created the NHS in 1948. Here he is shown meeting a patient at Papworth Hospital.

BUZZ BOX

By the 1960s, Britain did not have enough doctors and nurses to run its NHS services. To fill the gaps, many thousands of medical staff came from overseas to work in Britain.

THE WAY FORWARD

Britain still has its NHS and remains very proud of it. But the organisation has changed. Many of us now pay for some of its services, such as dentistry, eye tests and prescription medicines. Smaller and older hospitals have been closed. The new ones specialise in certain illnesses, so patients may have to travel long distances for treatment. Finally, because the NHS cannot possibly give everyone all the treatments they want, doctors proposed giving priority to certain cases, such as children and non-smokers.

▼ Surgeons repair the face of a person injured in a car crash.

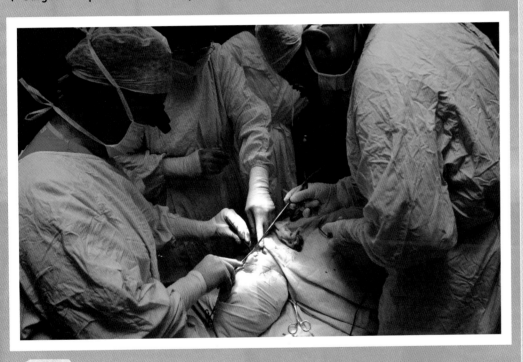

" The NHS? Yes, it was extraordinary. A woman came into the clinic with such a bad back, in such pain, that she was bent double all the time. She had not been able to afford treatment. "

Physiotherapist Marjorie Henderson in a conversation with the author, 2000.

THEN AND NOW

How long a person could be expected to live (life expectancy):

	1945	1965	1985	2004
Men	63.1	68.7	71.7	76.6
Women	68.1	74.6	77.4	81.0

TIMELINE

1948
National Health Service set up.

1952
Dental and prescription charges introduced.

1993
Private Finance Initiative (PFI) introduced, meaning private companies can build new hospitals and wards.

March 1998
NHS Direct, a nurse-led health advice service, is launched to give people 24-hour health advice over the phone.

2000
Private Public Partnership (PPP) introduced. The State and private companies build new hospitals and wards.

August 2004
Patient Choice gives patients waiting longer than six months for their operation a choice of a place for treatment.

By 1945 many of Britain's hospitals were old and in need of repair. Over the years, they were closed or modernised, and new ones built. The number of patients being treated grew, although they now spent much less time in hospital than they used to.

MILITARY DISCIPLINE

Hospitals in the 1940s and 50s were quite scary places. Visiting hours were limited. Husbands were not allowed to be with their wives when they gave birth. There were no bedside radios, TVs or phones. The large wards, each with long rows of beds on either side, were run with strict discipline by a ward sister. The hospital was organised like a pyramid, with the consultants (senior doctors) at the top, then the junior doctors, the sisters, the nurses and, finally, the patients.

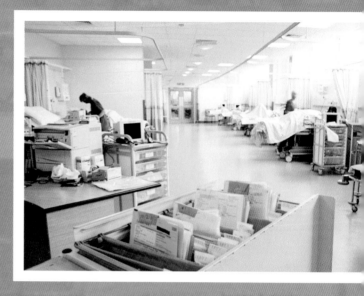

▲ A modern, well equipped hospital ward with nurses looking after patients.

CHANGE

By the 1960s, hospitals were changing fast. Patients' friends and relatives were allowed in more often. The buildings and equipment became more high-tech: spread around each hospital today, for instance, are machines to re-start a heart that has for some reason stopped beating. The wards grew smaller and the organisation less formal. Because medicines, treatments and equipment, such as body scanners, were more complicated, nursing changed. A nurse was no longer simply a kind, practical person with a smiling face and cheery word. The new nurses were highly-trained in medicine.

BUZZ BOX

As drugs became more powerful, hospital staff paid less attention to hygiene. Because of this, hospitals became home to fatal new 'superbugs', such as MRSA, that are very difficult to wipe out.

◀ Night Sister Shirley Bragg at work in 1965.

◀ Patients sit in a corridor at Broadmoor mental hospital in Berkshire, 1956.

MENTAL HEALTH

Our understanding of mental illness has changed enormously. In the 1940s, large numbers of mentally ill patients were locked away in bleak, isolated mental hospitals for years, sometimes for their entire lifetime. Such hospitals were known as 'lunatic asylums' or worse. Better drugs, treatments and understanding of mental illness allowed this practice to change. From the 1960s, many hospitals for the mentally ill were closed and their patients cared for in ordinary hospitals or, sometimes controversially, in the community.

> 66 *I used to go and hide in the toilets and lock the door, but the nurses used to fetch me ... down to ECT [electric shock treatment]. It was very frightening. After treatment I used to feel very tired and wanted to stay in bed. They used to lock me up sometimes because I used to scream.* 99

A patient named Winnie remembers her time in a mental hospital in 1953.

THEN AND NOW

For thousands of years nothing was known about a baby until it was born. By the 1970s ultrasound scanners could tell a mother whether her unborn child was a boy or a girl.

1979
The first BUPA (British United Provident Association) private hospital is opened.

1983
Mental Health Act extends rights of the mentally ill.

1987
Loud complaints that patients have to wait too long for hospital surgery.

1990
The Community Care Act allows patients with mental illness to be treated outside hospital. Unfortunately, not all of them were properly cared for.

1997
Labour government promises increases in hospital spending.

2006
Some parts of the NHS run into difficulties for spending too much money.

SURGERY

A hospital operation in the 1940s was a long and rather worrying business. By the 21st century this had largely changed. Most operations were quick and safe – and some wealthy people had surgery just to make themselves look younger!

SAFER AND SAFER

Surgery became safer for two main reasons. One was better anaesthetics, the drugs that put patients to sleep for an operation. In a modern operating theatre the patient is closely watched all the time and the amount of anaesthetic can be increased or reduced as necessary. The use of antibiotics, just starting in 1945, was a second reason why surgery was less dangerous. These new 'wonder drugs' killed off nearly all infections that might affect a wound after an operation.

NEW OPERATIONS

The twentieth century has been called the 'golden age of surgery' and the number of new operations that became possible after 1945 is remarkable. The most spectacular was transplant surgery, beginning with kidney transplants in 1954. Transplants became more reliable when doctors learned

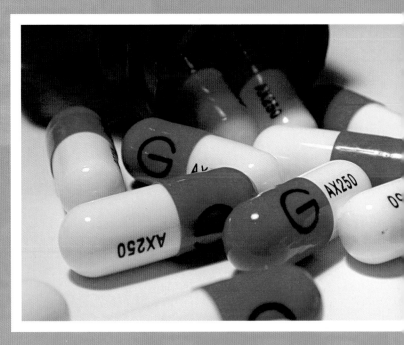

▲ A bottle of antibiotics prescribed by a doctor. These drugs help to kill off infection after surgery.

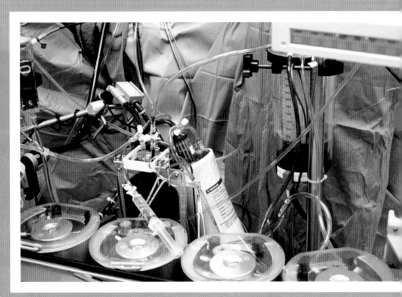

▲ A heart-lung machine. This machine is designed to take over the functions of the heart-lung system during heart surgery.

BUZZ BOX

In the past cancer was generally a fatal disease. Nowadays survival rates for many forms of cancer have risen thanks to a combination of surgery, drug treatment (chemotherapy) and radiotherapy.

how to stop the body 'rejecting' a transplanted organ. Equally dramatic were operations to repair damaged hearts and, from the 1960s onwards, replacing damaged joints with artificial ones. Later came 'keyhole surgery' – carrying out operations by making only tiny cuts in the body and working with a tiny TV camera. By 2007 surgeons could operate on the heart through a small hole in the patient's thigh!

COSMETIC SURGERY

During World War II surgeons working on patients badly burned in battle learned a good deal about reconstructing faces. They could 'graft' (move) skin from elsewhere in the body. This skill led to the rise of 'cosmetic surgery': expensive operations performed to alter the appearance of someone's face, tummy, breasts or other part of the body.

THEN AND NOW

After the removal of an appendix, in the 1950s patients were kept in bed for at least a week after the operation. Nowadays they are up and about in a matter of hours.

> " *I remember my step-father after he received his artificial hip in 1974. It was quite a new operation in those days. He was so pleased – like a new man. 'I can play golf again!' he smiled. 'It's a miracle!'* "
>
> Author's personal memory.

TIMELINE

1952
Doctors repair a human heart for the first time using a new valve.

1954
First kidney transplant.

1957
Reliable pacemaker developed.

1960
First hip replacement operation.

1962
Laser first used for eye surgery.

1967
First heart transplant.

1983
First successful heart and lung transplant.

1987
Brain tissue transplanted for the first time.

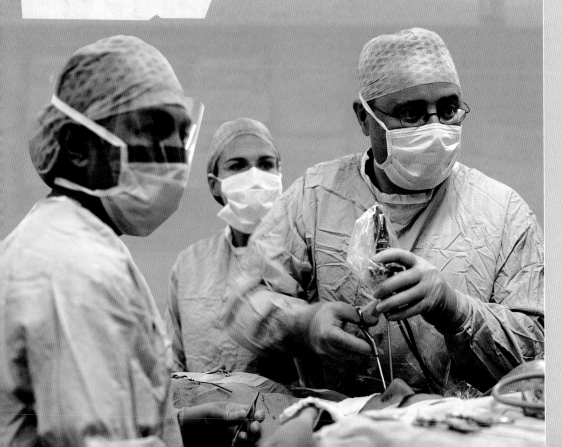

◀ An ENT (Ear, Nose and Throat) surgeon removes a growth using a pair of forceps (right hand). A computer helps him during the operation.

GOING TO THE DOCTOR

Visiting a doctor today is not very different from 60 years ago. One obvious difference is in the doctors themselves. In 1945 they were nearly all white and male. Nowadays they may well be female and from an ethnic minority, particularly Asian.

IN THE BEGINNING

In 1945, most family doctors (general practitioners or GPs) worked on their own or with a small group of other GPs. With the arrival of the NHS, these doctors were expected to treat all patients registered with them. The government paid them for their work. In some country areas there were not enough doctors to go around. Many were unhappy, saying they had too much work and not enough money.

STREAMLINING THE SERVICE

By the mid-1960s, the NHS had settled down and the GP system was operating quite well. Few doctors worked on their own now and practices had become larger. This meant that when patients went to see their family doctor they might be treated by another member of the practice. Not everyone liked this. The look of doctors' surgeries had changed little, although some were more cheerful and welcoming. The real change was that doctors had a vast range of new drugs to prescribe, from birth control pills to heart medicines.

> *"Our family doctor was Dr Myer Goldberg ... a personal friend to my grandparents and ... a very funny man ... [When] our neighbour ... Maggie Taylor ... was dying of cancer, ... Doctor Goldberg was at her side with her family to the end ... cracking jokes and swearing as usual. [He] was the greatest GP that I have ever met."*

Eric Gold's memories of life in the East End of London after World War II.

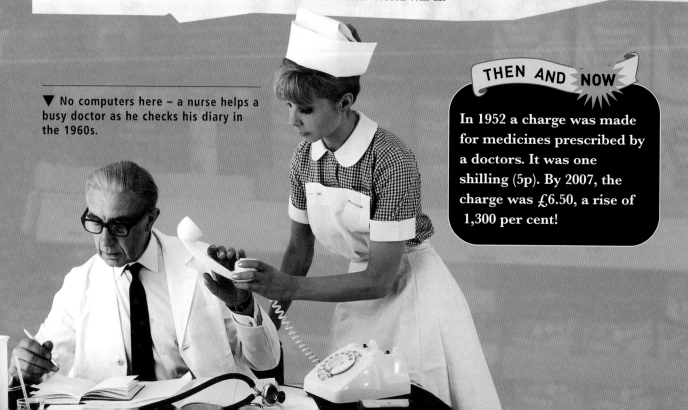

▼ No computers here – a nurse helps a busy doctor as he checks his diary in the 1960s.

THEN AND NOW

In 1952 a charge was made for medicines prescribed by a doctors. It was one shilling (5p). By 2007, the charge was £6.50, a rise of 1,300 per cent!

BUZZ BOX

At first, specialist doctors (consultants) did not like the NHS idea. They changed their minds only when they were allowed to work for the NHS as well as taking fees from private patients.

▲ Nowadays many GPs specialise in certain areas of care such as family planning.

GPS TODAY

By the 21st century, a GP's life had changed considerably. They could choose not to be called out to see a patient at night. Computers helped them spot illnesses and prescribe medicines. Other services, such as hospital Accident and Emergency centres and clinics, also lightened their burden of work. Doctors were paid to help prevent illnesses such as heart attack, cancer and diabetes as well as treat them. With people living longer, they found themselves spending more and more time with elderly patients.

▶A woman leaves a private medical centre. Patients can see a doctor or nurse without the need for an appointment.

1952
Royal College of General Practitioners established to set standards for GPs.

1974
The government reorganises the NHS to bring it closer to local communities.

1980s
Costs spiralling and patients waiting a long time for treatment.

1991-2
NHS reorganised again, setting up NHS Trusts.

2002
NHS reorganised again to make it more efficient.

2003
Doctors are given more freedom to choose when they work.

THE MARCH OF SCIENCE

Hospitals and surgeries, GPs and surgeons … all parts of our health service depend on science. Over the last 60 years, scientists have made amazing medical discoveries. As a result, some diseases have disappeared and many others can now be cured.

VACCINATION

In the 1940s, children often missed a few months of school because they caught common infectious diseases, such as mumps, measles and rubella (also known as German measles). Occasionally, these illnesses could be very serious. In the 1950s and 60s, vaccinations against these diseases were developed and today they are very rare. Vaccination also eliminated polio, a disease that often killed its victims or left them paralysed.

> 66 *At school I remember one boy, Nick, being really miserable. He said his dad had TB and had to go and live in a clinic and drink only orange juice. I didn't know what TB was, but I did know it was very serious. I think Nick's dad recovered.* 99
>
> **Author's personal memory.**

MEDICINES

The two biggest advances in the world of medical drugs were antibiotics and the contraceptive pill. The first antibiotic, penicillin, had been discovered before the war but it was available to doctors only in the 1940s. Later, other more powerful antibiotics were developed. These killed all kinds of germs. They could even fight the killer disease TB (tuberculosis). However, by the 1980s, doctors found some germs were resisting antibiotics.

The contraceptive pill became available in the 1960s. It allowed women, for the first time in history, safely and reliably to decide whether or not to start a family.

▲ After suffering from polio, new mother Mrs Dawn Varma could breathe only with the help of an 'iron lung' machine.

BUZZ BOX

The 1973 film *The Boys from Brazil* was about a scientist who made new Adolf Hitlers by cloning. Today, with advances in cloning technology, this scary idea is not so far-fetched.

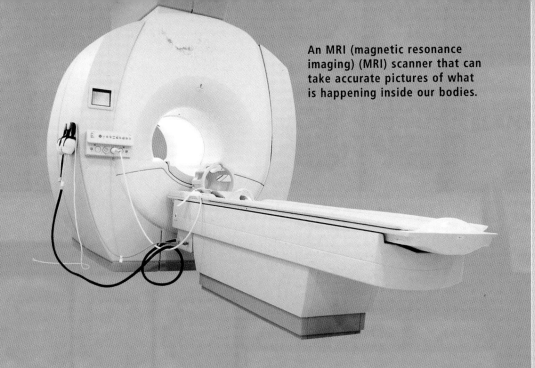

An MRI (magnetic resonance imaging) (MRI) scanner that can take accurate pictures of what is happening inside our bodies.

TIMELINE

1946
Antibiotics first used.

1953
DNA discovered.

1955
Effective polio vaccine introduced.

1961
Contraceptive pill available.

1972
Computers used in scanning the body.

1997
Dolly the Sheep, the first cloned animal, is born.

2004
British scientists allowed to clone human tissue.

NEW TECHNOLOGY

By the 21st century, scientists were exploring new and mysterious frontiers. Their work was based on the discovery, in 1953, of DNA – the basic building blocks of all life. Gradually, scientists realised that our genes differ in small but important ways from person to person. A person's genes can carry an illness or a high chance of getting that illness. Could we, the doctors wondered, treat people by altering their genes?

▼Two identical rabbits that have been produced by cloning. Scientists hope to use cloning to make 'spare parts' for humans.

THEN AND NOW

In the 1940s, many couples remained childless. Today this is much more rare because doctors have developed new techniques of helping women conceive.

The story of our health since 1945 has not been all rosy. True, there have been remarkable improvements and we now live longer and more pain-free lives than we did. Yet illness and sickness remain and there are signs that some people's health is getting worse, not better.

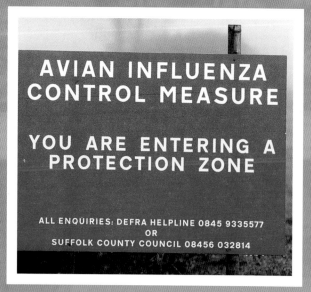

▲ Take care! A warning sign near a farm where turkeys were found to have 'Bird Flu' in 2006.

VIRUSES

HIV is caused by a virus. Viruses are harder to treat than germs because they are not affected by antibiotics and they continually change. As with polio, vaccinations may work. However, finding a suitable vaccination is very difficult and there are still no reliable vaccinations against diseases such as HIV, the common cold and many types of flu. In the winter of 2006-7 Britain was alarmed by fears that a new type of killer flu – 'Bird Flu' – might be brought in by wild birds.

▲ Please give! A man collects money for the Terrence Higgins HIV/AIDS charity.

HIV

In the late 1970s, a few doctors began worrying about people dying of a mysterious illness that destroyed the body's built-in defence system. Later, the disease was identified as the HIV virus. It killed millions of people worldwide and ruined the lives of many millions more. By 2005, 63,500 Britons had HIV, although 20 per cent of them did not realise it. At least 17,300 people had died of the disease. There were drugs that slowed down the disease but there was no cure.

BUZZ BOX

In 1918-9, just after World War I (1914-1918), flu killed more people than had died in the war. Scientists are afraid that the same sort of disaster could happen again if a new type of flu virus appears.

LIFESTYLE DISEASES

Viruses were not the only worry. As we became richer and food became cheaper, the British put on weight. Many people's health began to get worse as a result of their diet By 2007, we were the fattest nation in Europe. We also took less exercise. As a result of our diet and this lack of exercise, our health grew worse and illnesses like heart attack, stroke and diabetes increased. Experts suggested that unless something was done, people's expectation of life could start to fall.

◄ Too many chips? A boy is tested to see if he is too fat (obese).

THEN AND NOW

In the 1940s, cigarettes were advertised as being a good for you because they helped weight loss. By the 1970s each packet of cigarettes carried a warning that smoking was dangerous.

TIMELINE

1950s
Scientists begin to link smoking to cancer.

1971
Health warnings appear on cigarette packets.

1984
HIV identified.

1985
Alcohol units introduced to help sensible drinking.

2005
British doctors talking of an 'obesity epidemic'.

2006
Scotland bans smoking in enclosed public places. The rest of the UK follows in 2007.

2007
Bird Flu reaches Britain.

HARD TIMES

The last 60 years have seen a revolution in what, when and where we eat. In 1945 Britain was still at war. The range of foods available was very limited and many were scarce. This changed slowly over the next 15 years, when our diet (the food and drink we consume and the effects it has on us) started to alter.

RATIONING

Britain cannot grow all the food it needs. Some has to come from overseas, mostly in ships. Before and during World War II cargo ships were needed for war purposes and enemy submarines sank many of them. Food supplies ran low. So everyone had enough, the government rationed many foods – allowing only a fixed amount for each person. The sort of foods that were rationed were meat, sweets, butter, bacon, milk, jam and biscuits. Fish, sausages, potatoes and home-grown vegetables, like carrots and cabbage, were not rationed. Oranges, bananas and other luxuries from overseas were unavailable. Interestingly, rationing forced people to eat sensibly and the health of the nation improved.

The average ration for fresh eggs during World War II was 3 eggs per person per week – nowadays it is common for people to have two eggs each day for breakfast!

BACK TO NORMAL

Rationing continued long after the war. In fact, bread was rationed for the first time in 1946 – after the war had ended. Sweets did not come 'off rations', allowing people to buy as much as they could afford, until 1953; bananas were not freely available for another year. Even then, the British diet was much less varied than today. Much of what we ate was fresh, because there were almost no freezers and not many families had fridges.

▶ A selection of ration books.

▲ During rationing, "exotic" foods such as bananas were off the menu in Britain.

> 66 *A teacher told me that one day, before I started school, these odd yellow fruits appeared for school lunch. The children had never seen them before. They were bananas! The teacher showed us how to open them – then told the children to save the skins so they could be sent back for re-filling!* 99

Personal memory of the author.

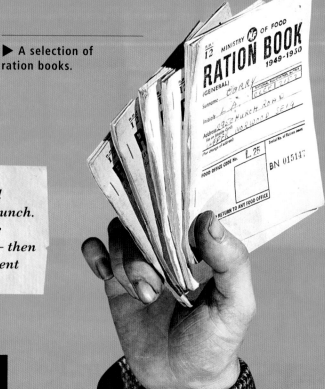

▲ A fish and chip stall in Scarborough, Yorkshire, 1952.

TIMELINE

1939-45
World War II – many foods rationed.

1946
Bread rationed for the first time.

1948
Bread and flour come off the rationing list.

1950s
Fridges begin to become commonplace in many households

1952
End of tea rationing.

1954
Rationing finally ends. Bacon and other meats are the last items to be taken off the rationing list.

SIMPLE FOOD

Apart from fish and chips, or bacon and eggs in a café, in the 1950s eating out at a restaurant was only for the well-off. There were almost no Indian or Chinese restaurants. Most people ate simple meals of meat, potatoes and vegetables. A burger was something Americans ate and almost no one knew what a pizza was.

BUZZ BOX

When they opened in the 1950s, Wimpey bars were so cool! They had started in the US and served American-style food like hamburgers and 'fries'.

From the mid 50s, British eating habits began to change fast. Different foods appeared on our tables, cooking became easier and we developed a huge appetite for snacks. As nearly all homes had a TV, the dining table made way for meals in comfy chairs before the 'box'.

▲ A new way to shop: one of the first supermarkets, Maidenhead, 1954.

FOREIGN FOODS

There were several reasons for the British diet becoming more varied. One was the arrival in the UK of thousands of immigrants from India, Pakistan and Bangladesh. Many of them opened reasonable-priced curry restaurants – and British quickly developed a taste for spicy Asian food. Supermarkets, which sprang up in the 1950s, offered new items, such as avocado pears, that small grocers had not sold. Cheap air travel and overseas holidays introduced people to new dishes. From the US came burgers and an appetite for Italian pizza.

ALL THE YEAR ROUND

Another big change came about because most foods became available all the year round. We forgot about 'seasonal foods'. Strawberries, for example, which previously could be found only in the summer, were now flown in to Britain all the year round. The same applied to tomatoes and many other fruits and vegetables.

BUZZ BOX

It is said that pizza caught on after soldiers first tasted it while fighting in Italy during World War II – and when they returned home they wanted more.

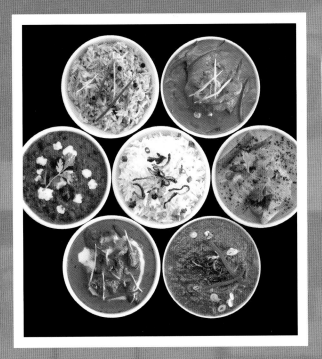

> **"** *Indian restaurants were quite new in the 1960s. We loved our local Kashmir – a plate of Bombay potatoes for one shilling and sixpence (7.5 p) was all we students could afford – but it filled us up.* **"**
>
> Personal memories of the author.

▲ Tasty dishes from Asia have made British meal times more exciting.

TIMELINE

1950
Britain has 50 self-service supermarkets.

1954
Food rationing finally ends.

1956
First Tesco self-service supermarkets opens.

First TV dinner sold.

1967
First microwave sold.

2007
The film *Fast Food Nation* changes the way many people think about the food they eat.

FINGERS AND NUGGETS

In 1945 very little of the food was 'processed' and flavourings and colourings were quite rare. To have an apple pie, for instance, one bought the ingredients for the pastry and the filling, and made the pie at home.

Ready-made dishes were available, but they were expensive. By the 1980s, that had all changed. Frozen food, dried food and tinned food filled the supermarket shelves. Pre-cooked meals saved time and effort. Fish was made into fingers, turkey into twizzlers, chicken into nuggets – all with huge lists of strange ingredients. Sometimes we hardly knew what we were eating.

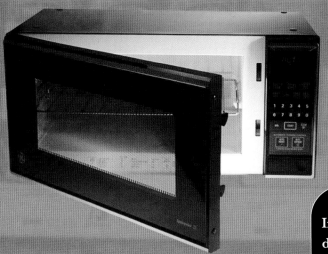

▲ A microwave from the 1980s. This device enabled people to cook pre-prepared, frozen meals quickly and easily.

THEN AND NOW

In the 1940s and 50s Britain was a nation of beer drinkers. Wine was drunk only by wealthy, smart people. This began to change in the 1960s. Today Britain is one of the world's main wine consumers.

GOING GREEN

By the 1980s, the British were starting to wonder about what they were eating. What were its ingredients? Had it been healthily and kindly produced? Had the farmers been treated fairly? Very slowly, what was eaten and how it was produced began to change.

WORRIED CONSUMERS

After the war food production became steadily more industrial. Animals raised for food never saw the daylight. They were fed with unsuitable substances to make them grow faster and stay healthy. Tons of fertiliser were tipped onto the soil to increase yields. Food products were laced with preservatives, colourings and flavourings. There were scandals: experts said artificial ingredients affected children's behaviour. African farmers starved while their produce filled our shelves. Cows caught BSE ('mad cow disease') when fed with mashed up animal parts – and over 150 Britons died of the disease.

ORGANIC

By the 1990s, a small number of shoppers were rebelling against what was happening. They demanded organic produce, grown without any chemicals. Farmers' markets appeared where shoppers could buy produce straight from the farm. Several companies insisted that those who grew the crops they used were paid a fair price. In time the supermarkets caught on to the new mood and started selling their own organic and fair trade products. Labels had to state clearly what was in a product.

▲ A cow suffering from BSE, a horrible disease of the nerves.

THEN AND NOW

Until the 1990s, there were few laws about how food should be labelled. Then the following law was introduced:
'All food ... shall be marked or labelled with—
   (a) the name of the food;
   (b) a list of ingredients; ...
   (d) any special storage conditions or conditions of use;
   (e) the name ... of (i) the manufacturer or packer ...'
From the Government food labelling law, 1996.

❝ *During the 70s we were not aware how badly some children were affected by sugar, additives, colouring and sugar substitutes ... I only became aware of this when my son Oliver had his first taste of Coco Cola – his behaviour changed immediately and became almost manic ...* ❞

American food specialist Dr Ben Feingold.

GM CROPS

During the 1990s, scientists learned to make new crops by arranging their genetic make up. This was known as 'genetic modification' (GM). When Britain experimented with them, there were protests. Eventually, GM crops were allowed in America but not in Europe. They yielded more food, however, and by the 21st century British farmers found it hard to produce food as cheaply as those overseas. To help, they were paid to look after the countryside as well as farm it.

◀ Organic vegetable boxes, delivered to the home, became popular in the 1990s.

▲ Greenpeace protesters stage a rally in a field with GM crops near Norfolk.

BUZZ BOX

In 2007, there was a suspected outbreak of bird flu in Norfolk. As a result, 35,000 birds were slaughtered to prevent the outbreak spreading. Scientific tests then proved that 2,500 turkeys at the Bernard Matthews farm died of the deadly H5N1 virus. 159,000 more birds were slaughtered as a result. Some people believed the disease came from imported carcasses from the firm's plant in Hungary, where birds also tested positive for the virus.

TIMELINE

1946
The Soil Association was founded in 1946 by a group of farmers, scientists and nutritionists who observed a direct connection between farming practice and environmental health.

1980s
CJD or 'Mad Cow Disease' spreads in Britain.

1984
Government report blames intensive agriculture for the terrible damage to British wildlife, including the destruction of 95 per cent of wildflower meadows.

1990s
First organic food market set up at Spitalfields, London

1992
First GM food, a type of tomato, produced.

2004
The government says that farms will not grow GM crops.

In 1945 there were few places to eat out in a typical town centre. There was perhaps a wartime 'British restaurant', a café, an hotel, a fish and chip shop and, maybe, a restaurant. Compare that with a town today – what a change!

▲ Today there are fast food chains in most towns throughout Britain.

▲ Posh restaurants such as The Ivy in London grew increasingly popular in the 1990s.

FAST FOOD

Over the last sixty years, fast food restaurants have exploded across the country. Once we had just fish and chip shops. In the 1950s, a new type of fast food restaurant appeared. These burger bars mushroomed from the 1970s onwards. They were popular because they sold cheap and reasonably tasty food without frills at all times of the day. Most were self-service and used disposable dishes and no cutlery. The menus were limited and rarely changed, but the quality was consistent. Only in the 1990s did doctors begin to consider fast food unhealthy.

QUALITY FOOD

Britain's growing wealth allowed millions to eat out. While many were happy with burgers and fries, others tried more interesting dishes. These

> " In the '50s my mother worked at a restaurant ... on Cambridge Street [Sheffield]. The policy ... was for the waitresses to salvage any pieces of meat left over from dirty plates being cleared away, which was ... used in the next day's stew. My mother was fired for refusing to do this. "
>
> Memories of 'jmdee', 2007.

After World War II cod was a cheap, everyday fish: 'cod and chips' in newspaper was the usual serving from a 'chippie'. Overfishing means that today cod is seen as an expensive luxury!

included Indian, Chinese and other Oriental meals, kebabs and pizzas – either eaten in or taken away. Most pubs, which had previously served just drinks and salty snacks, now offered cooked meals. The number of quality restaurants also grew. In the 1950s, Britain's food was famous for being dull and tasteless. By the 21st century, it was as good as anywhere.

TV COOKS

Britain's 'food revolution' was helped by a new star – the 'TV chef'! The earliest was the formidable Fanny Cradock, who began broadcasting in the 1950s. In the 1970s came the most famous TV cook of all, Delia Smith.

Her programmes and books helped change the way the nation thought about food. By the 21st century, cooking and restaurant programmes were shown every day. Their hosts – like Jamie Oliver, Madhur Jaffrey, Nigella Lawson and Gordon Ramsey – were top-rank celebrities.

BUZZ BOX

The Michelin Guide, the most famous restaurant guide, did not even list British restaurants until 1974. It then gave stars (for exceptional food) to only 25 places. By 2007 this had risen to 108.

▶ Jamie Oliver was just one of a number of celebrity chefs promoting healthy eating in the 21st century.

TIMELINE

1952
Fanny Cradock becomes Britain's first TV chef.

1973
Cookery expert Delia Smith first appears on TV.

1974
Britain's first McDonald's opens.

1982
Le Gavroche becomes Britain's first restaurant to win three Michelin stars.

2005
The *European Restaurant Magazine* reveals that 14 of the top 50 restaurants in Europe are in Britain.

2006
Celebrity chef Jamie Oliver launches campaign for healthier school meals.

What are we to make of all the changes to our health and diet over the last sixty years? In many ways we have seen progress, improving health and better and more interesting food. But new difficulties have arisen, as they always will.

▲ It is now quite common for people to live to the age of 80 – and beyond.

▲ Binge drinking is a serious problem in 21st-century Britain.

PLUS ...

The British people are living longer than ever before. There are two reasons for this: greater wealth and advances in medicine. There is vastly more food available than in 1945, and most of us can afford to eat more of it. Medical science has found cures for many diseases and better treatments for others. It has also discovered the harmful effects of certain lifestyle habits, such as smoking.

... AND MINUS

Nevertheless, we still have our difficulties. Many of us eat and drink too much – by the 21st century, 'binge drinking', especially among young people, had become a serious problem. Heart disease and diabetes, both associated with being overweight, were increasing. Our health would improve if we exercised more, but cars, TV and the PC have made us lazy. Some people refuse to stop smoking, although they know it will kill

In the 1940s, there were very few cars and almost no TVs. It was usual for children to spend hours on summer evenings and at weekends playing football in the street. Far fewer children do this now.

them. Science itself has raised tricky questions: Who can tell what the long-term effects of GM food will be? Do we really want doctors to 'grow' spare parts for our bodies?

THE FUTURE

Medical scientists say that one day they will have cures for almost all diseases, even cancer and HIV, and they will have drugs to stop us overeating. Some claim that they will be able to slow down the process of aging, too, making it possible for everyone to live to over 100. If the changes over the last 60 years have been dramatic, those over the next 100 may be even more so.

> *" The positive trends in recent decades in combating heart disease, partly the consequence of the decline in smoking, will be reversed. Indeed, this will be the first generation where children die before their parents as a consequence of childhood obesity. "*
>
> *The Guardian, 27 May 2004*

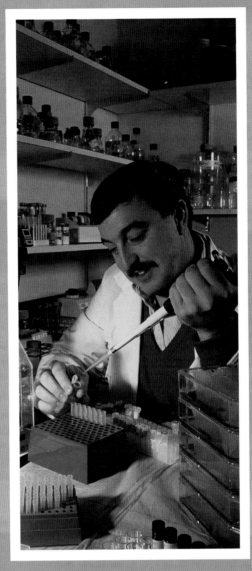

▲ Scientists hope that soon we will be able to wipe out diseases like cancer.

BUZZ BOX

Do health and wealth make us happy? A 1999-2000 survey found Britain 24th in the world happiness league. At the top were three nations that are not especially healthy or wealthy: Nigeria, Mexico and Venezuela.

TIMELINE

1948
Life expectancy for men is 63 and for women 68.

1950
Chemotherapy invented – a great breakthrough for tackling many forms of cancer.

1957
British researchers say that smoking definitely causes lung cancer.

1992
First nicotine skin patch available to help smokers quit.

2004
Life expectancy for men risen to 76 and for women 81.

2007
A team at Moorfields Eye Hospital, London, carry out the world's first gene therapy operation to cure blindness in children and young adults.

GLOSSARY

antibiotic	powerful germ-killing drug
clone	exact genetic copy of something
consultant	doctor who specialises in a branch of medicine
consumer	anyone who buys things
diabetes	disease where certain glands do not work properly
DNA	basic material of living cells
epidemic	widespread outbreak of disease
gene	part of DNA that determines who we are
GM	Genetically modified: made by scientifically arranging genes of other plants
GP	General Practitioner, a family doctor
graft	take skin from one part of the body and use it elsewhere
HIV	the virus that causes AIDS, a disease thatdestroys the body's defences against infection
immigrant	person who enters another country to live there
linoleum	hard plastic flooring
NHS	National Heath Service
obese	seriously overweight
organic	food grown without the aid of artificial chemicals
overfishing	taking too much fish from the sea
pacemaker	small machine that controls the heartbeat
polio	disease that destroys the body's nerves
practice	where GPs work
prescription	medicine that can be given only by doctors
processed	manufactured
rationing	making sure everyone gets their fair share of important or luxury foods and goods
scanner	machine that can look inside the body
tuberculosis	killer lung disease
ultrasound	type of scanner that uses very small sound waves
vaccination	means of protecting a person against a disease
ward	large hospital bedroom

FURTHER INFORMATION
Books to read

Arthur Marwick, British Society Since 1945, Penguin, 2003

Kenneth O. Morgan, Britain Since 1945, Oxford, 2001

Gill and Mike Corbishley, Appetite for Change: Food and Cooking in the 20th Century, English Heritage, 1993

Richard Tames, Penicillin: A Breakthrough in Medicine, Heinemann, 2006

Stewart Ross, Britain Since 1930, Evans, 2003

Sally Hewitt, The 1970s (I Can remember), Franklin Watts, 2003

Jane Shuter, Britain Since 1930, Heinemann, 2005

WEBSITES
www.bbc.co.uk/history/british/modern/overview_1945_present_01

www.ageconcern.org.uk/TimeCapsule/1950s_D8A72E0B8C8641E6922CABF7 07CE7747 (follow links to time capsules of similar Age Concern sites for other decades)

www.great-britain.co.uk/history/post45

www.historylearningsite.co.uk/medical_changes_from_1945

PLACES TO VISIT
London has many museums related to medicine – see www.medicalmuseums.org

Science Museum, London

Tayside Medical History Museum, Dundee

Your local museum

Note to parents and teachers: Every effort has been made by the Publishers to ensure that these websites are suitable for children, that they are of the highest educational value, and that they contain no inappropriate or offensive material. However, because of the nature of the Internet, it is impossible to guarantee that the contents of these sites will not be altered. We strongly advise that Internet access is supervised by a responsible adult.

INDEX

additives, food 21, 22
AIDS 16
antibiotics 10, 14, 15, 16, 28
Avian Flu 16, 17

BSE 22, 23

cancer 10, 12, 13, 17, 27
cloning 14, 15, 27, 28
contraceptive pill 12, 14, 15, 27
crops 22, 23
   GM 23, 27, 28

dentists 6, 7
DNA 15, 27, 28
diabetes 13, 17, 26, 28
discoveries, medical 14-15, 26
doctors 6, 7, 8, 12-13, 14, 16, 17, 24, 27
drinking (alcohol) 7, 17, 19, 26, 27
drugs 9, 10, 12, 14, 27

eating habits 18-21
eating out 19, 20, 21, 24, 25

farming 22-23
fast food 18, 20, 21, 24, 25
fish and chips 18, 19, 24, 25
food 17, 18-23, 26
foreign 19, 20, 25
organic 22, 23, 28
flu 16, 17

GP (general practitioner) 10, 12-13, 14, 28

heart disease 10, 11, 13, 17, 26
HIV 16, 17, 27, 28
hospitals 6, 7, 8-9, 10, 11, 13, 14, 28

illnesses 6, 7, 8-9, 10, 12, 13, 14, 15, 16, 17

life-expectancy 7, 16, 17

medicines 6, 7, 12, 14, 26 see also
drugs

NHS (National Health Service) 6-7, 12,
   13, 27, 28
nurses 7, 8, 9

prescriptions 7, 10, 12, 28

obesity 17, 26, 27, 28
operations 6, 10, 11

rationing (food) 18, 19, 21, 28
restaurants 19, 20, 24-25

scientists 14-15, 23, 26, 27
smoking 17, 26
supermarkets 19, 20, 21, 22, 23, 27
surgery 7, 9, 10-11, 14

transplants 10, 11

vaccination 7, 14, 15, 16, 27, 28
viruses 16, 17

Wimpey 18, 21